MW01031523

To Margo

Kate Sullivan

Smoke + mirrors

WRITTEN & ILLUSTRATED BY

Kate Sullivan

SULLYARTS
www.sullyarts.com

ISBN 978-1-304-49965-3

ACKNOWLEDGMENTS
The author wishes to thank the editors of the publications in which the following poems and essays first appeared: *Ode to a Teardrop*, Rush Literary Magazine; *There But for the Grace of God, I'll Fly Away, Aunt Joan, On the Road*, Writers.com; The Dillydoun Review; *Black Ice*, Loud Coffee Press; *Lost at Cousin Jackie's*, Irish Central; *Mudlarking at the Beauport*, Sleet Magazine, Piano Lessons, *Defenestration*

Illustrations by Kate Sullivan
Design by Kate Sullivan & Jeff Mellin (jeffmellin.com)

FIRST EDITION

SULLYARTS
www.sullyarts.com

FOR MY CHILDREN
who made me

&

FOR BILL
*my husband, my friend,
my rock*

also by Kate Sullivan

CDs

Beane Family Christmas
Nine Lives
Like a Child
Lettres de Paris
Lenya!

THEATER PIECES

Lenya! The Love of Kurt Weill
Piaf, the little Sparrow

ART EXHIBITS

Birds in High Places
Second Story Theater Portraits
It's a Dog's Life

PICTURE BOOKS

On Linden Square
What Do You Hear?

MUSIC COMPOSITION

Pinocchio, for string quartet
The Three Fates, for strings
The Pied Piper, for orchestra
Sweeney Astray, for chamber orchestra and chorus
Fanfare for the Common Woman, for chamber orchestra

Our unconscious mind...is a storehouse of relics and memories of the past.

— C. G. *Jung*

contents

smoke + mirrors

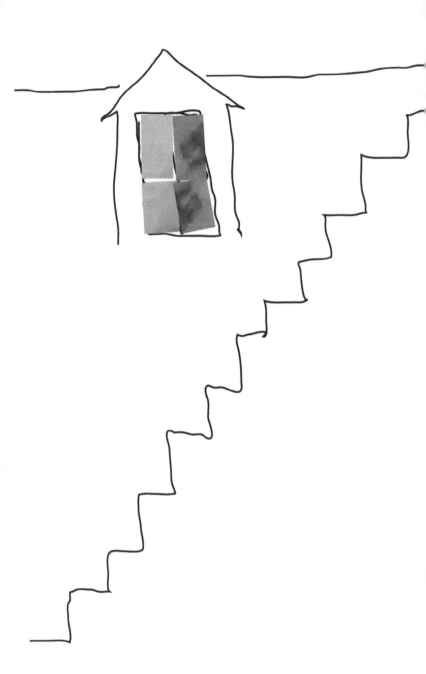

homesick

I CHOP DILL FOR DINNER and smell the melancholy of the
sleepy seaside summer beach house of my childhood friend.
The weather-worn front stairs lead from the hot pavement to
the wide porch, scattered with tired wicker chairs. I remember
the mystery of the hinged window seat on the ocean side, where
they kept an enormous box kite, hand-made with lumber, not
sticks. They ate dinner at a specified time, everyone seated
at the table like it was a Sunday. One by one, we passed our
empty plates to her father at the head of the table. He would
serve, asking if you wanted the turnip, the corned beef, the
potato, while all nine of them watched. They used washcloths
and knew how to sail. They played board games and said the
rosary after dinner. Then, in the deepening dusk, my friend and
I would head upstairs to the squeaky twin beds on the third
floor, the smell of dill drifting in the dormer window.

on the road

OBJECTS AT REST WILL STAY AT REST and objects in motion will stay in a straight-line motion unless acted upon by an unbalanced force.

My great grandmother, Mary Somers was born in 1852 in County Limerick, Ireland. She emigrated to New Britain, Connecticut with her family when she was nine years old. She went to school until she was eleven and then went to work. At age 16, she had a fight with her mother, took whatever money she had and went down to the train station where she placed half of it on the counter and bought a one-way ticket for as far as the money would take her. The conductor told her to get off in Cleveland. She knocked on the door of the local rectory and told them, "I'm Mary Somers and I'm a seamstress." They found her a home with the O'Briens. She married John O'Brien The Mover, became the vet for the horses and had ten children — one of them, my grandfather.

Dumb luck, pure chance, disasters, miracles. Solid turns to liquid, liquid turns to gas. And in a leap of faith and science, solid turns to gas.

Mad King Sweeney was an Irish king who ruled the roost in Medieval Ireland. A renegade, prone to losing his temper, impulsive and lawless, he would fly off the handle at the drop of a hat. He had a fight with Ronan Finn, the local cleric. He threw Ronan's hymnal into the lake. Oh, an otter fished it out all right, but Ronan cursed Sweeney, turned him into a bird, and banished him to roam the rocky crags of Northern Ireland. Sweeney lost his home, his wife, his friends and was forced into a life of bitter self-examination. He was set adrift from all known places. Isolated in his tree-top dwelling, he lamented his fate, became an observer, a philosopher.

In search of wholeness, we take journeys we might not want to take. Everything is in constant flux.

Everyone is moving from one state to another, from liquid to solid to gas, from Ohio to São Miguel, from Lampedusa to Akron. The swallows and butterflies gather in clouds of frenzy for their trek South.

This one is getting married, that one is leaving a group of childhood friends. Life is ebb and flow. We strike it rich! We lose what we thought was a sure thing. We make one small decision that changes everything; to buy a house by the sea, to enter the convent, to take that teaching job in Korea. Or perhaps, even if we do none of these things, we are nevertheless changed by simply walking through life. And like a balloon, which never returns to its original state once inflated, we never return to those roads not taken.

We can't fully understand our lives as we are living them. The meaning appears later. An old Irish saying goes, *Is maith an scéalaí an aimsir*. Time is the great storyteller. The Goths headed South, the Visigoths headed East, the Hondurans are headed North, the Conestoga wagons headed West.

For every action there is an opposite and equal reaction.

On the Day of the Absent Ipalans, in a small town in Guatemala, townsfolk celebrate those who strike out for a better life. Jennifer Sagastume, who lives with her house-cleaner mother in Maryland, came back a few years ago to be crowned *Queen of the Absent Ipalans*. She is proof of a

better life in a promised land. But she also speaks to another dream: the possibility of return and perhaps the possibility of never having to leave.

The world is made up of leavers and stayers. Leavers set out for adventure, for safety, for growth, fame, fortune, freedom. Stayers stay for stability, for fear, for family, friends. Rilke knew them both,

> Sometimes a man stands up during supper and walks
> outdoors, and keeps on walking, because of a church
> that stands somewhere in the East. And his children say
> blessings on him as if he were dead. And another man,
> who remains inside his own house, stays there, inside the
> dishes and in the glasses, so that his children have to go
> far out into the world toward that same church, which he forgot.

We all do the best we can with what we know at the time. It's rather odd how we're not tuned in to the stories of our ancestors until we become ancient ourselves!

And, no matter what we decide, perhaps we all end up a bit wistful for *things we have done and things we have left undone.*

ode to a teardrop

I AM NOT A POET, but give me a choice between an acrobatic clarinet line and a piece of dry toast, I'll take the clarinet every time. Maybe that counts for something, and I'd rather sing than talk. Remember the time I had to wipe my tears on the wide, white sleeves of my surplus when we sang that Irish tune during the service? Or when we would jump over each other to be chosen by Mrs. Keenan (requiescat in pace) to go to the blackboard to scan the dactyls and spondees of the iambic pentameter of Virgil? *Forsan et haec olim meminisse iuvabit.* Perhaps someday it will be pleasing to remember these things. I bought the sheet music for Rhapsody in Blue in Newton Center over a half century ago, when I was a junior in high school and have been working on it ever since. And to think he made it all up! And I believe I've slipped through life without ever having read a sonnet. What a shame, but alas, choices must be made. Now 70 winters have besieged my brow, but 70 is the new 50 and I'm hoping to take a cross-country trip like my whizz-bang 72-year old poetry teacher, Barbara.

Maybe I'll get one of those little silver teardrop trailers, big enough for one bed and a toilet and a place to heat water for tea. I could read my sestinas in little country taverns, then park my teardrop at the water's edge for a skinny dip before cocktails. "You're only young once!" my father used to say, and at 70, he took us all by surprise by dying suddenly and peacefully in his sleep. "A gift from the angels!" said one old lady at the party back at the house. I was 34 and wanted to clock her one.

Now I know she was right.

back to
school

A *is for Astigmatism.* I had a lazy eye. I was supposed to do daily exercises, holding up two pencils, one close to my nose, the other a foot away from my face. Focus on one, then the other. One, then the other. This was to train both eyes to work at the same time. They never have. I have somehow adapted. My right eye still drifts out to the side when I'm not using it. Marty Feldman is my hero.

B *is for Bankruptcy* (see midlife crisis, zoning). It was the late '80s, a heady time for real estate investors. Interest rates were low, house values were headed up. Fast. I got a job as a Latin teacher, but quit so I could make a million bucks. My first husband and I bought, rehabbed and sold many houses and made lots of money. It was all very heady until the market came to a screeching halt. We declared bankruptcy in some courthouse somewhere. We lost everything, including our house. The Sears representative was there to say we could keep our vacuum cleaner. Homeless, with four children and a vacuum cleaner.

C *is for the chèvre* that my new husband and I made, after bumping down a long dirt road to find the lady who owned some goats. After asking countless puzzled grocery store clerks for the rennet we were supposed to have, we found The Cheese Lady in western Mass. She had everything a know-nothing-cheese-maker could ever desire.

$\mathcal{D}$ *is for Diabetes.* Our fourth child, Olivia, was diagnosed with Type 1 diabetes when she was 17. It was a strong reminder of what matters in life. Life, in fact, matters in life.

$\mathcal{E}$ *is for Epiphone,* my first electric guitar. I don't know what possessed me to buy it, but it started me on a long quest to learn jazz. I set down my folk guitar and went for the twang of electricity. I eventually went back to the smooth, jazzy sound of my first guitar, newly equipped with an electric pick-up. I gave the Epiphone to my son, Owen. He was going to trade it in on another guitar. We would have gotten a needed $400 on the trade-in. The salesman said, "Don't sell this guitar. It's too special." Owen still has it. He's keeping it just in case either of us want to play the blues.

$\mathcal{F}$ *is for Forgiveness.* The older I get, the more I know that we all make mistakes. We all hurt others, sometimes unintentionally, sometimes not. We all need to forgive and to be forgiven.

$\mathcal{G}$ *is for Grapevine.* My second husband and I moved to a little falling-down house on a river. We chased out the water rats, knocked out a lot of walls and built a pergola, where we grew grapes to make our own wine. It was terrible.

$\mathcal{H}$ *is for the handwriting analyst* who told me I often anticipate resistance to my ideas. I don't know what the hell she's talking about.

$\mathcal{I}$ *is for Ireland.* My grandparents were born in Ireland. When I found out that qualified me for Irish citizenship, I travelled to Ireland to find my Grampa Tim's birth certificate. I probably could have found it on line. Going to Ireland was more fun.

J *is for the Jujube candies* we ate in the dark at The Community Playhouse in Wellesley Hills. Movies cost 25 cents...*Ben Hur, The Parent Trap, Snow White and the Seven Dwarfs.* We were all very upset that the cost for *The Shaggy Dog* increased to 35 cents.

K *is for the Kremlin Chamber Orchestra,* which played the piece I entered in their Mozart 250 competition. A fugue was required. I wrote a fugue of sorts. At the rehearsal, when Maestro Rachlevsky turned to ask me if I approved of their rendition of my piece, I managed to say yes, even though I thought I might faint. For the performance that evening, I sat in the balcony, just to drink it all in. I didn't realize that the Maestro would turn after each piece to ask the composer to take a bow. When he came to me, he couldn't find me. I sang a loud *YOO HOO* from up in the peanut gallery. And so now, I can also say that I sang in Carnegie Hall.

L *is for Latin* that I studied for many years. It is deep in my bones. *De gustibus non est disputandum.*

M *is for the Midlife Crisis* that was triggered by losing all our money. (see *B is for Bankruptcy*) I began to think that perhaps spending time just going after money was a waste of a life.

N *is for Nudity.* See skinny dips.

O *is for the outboard motor* on the 14' boat at Lake Sunapee. My seventeenth summer, I waitressed at a restaurant across the lake. I took the boat to work. That same summer, I met my husband, who came in for a sandwich.

P *is for puppet.* I've never met a puppet I didn't like; hand puppets, marionettes, shadow puppets. I spent a week once as the resident composer at a puppetry conference at The Eugene O'Neil Theatre in New London, Ct., where puppeteers from all over came to show off their creations. I ate lunch one day with a woman and her daughter who put cooked lobster legs and claws on their fingers and began a lobster dance at the table. They turned out to be Jim Henson's widow and daughter.

Q *is for how my Cape Cod husband pronounces quahog —* kwo-hog, not the land-lubbers co-hog.

R *is for regurgitate or throw up.* I will do anything NOT to throw up.

S *is for skinny dip.* There is no greater feeling than slipping through the water with nothing on.

T *is for the tubal ligation* I had when the narcissistic boyfriend I happened upon after 25 years of marriage and 4 babies, wanted me to have his baby.

U *is for the ultrasound* that showed that my fourth baby was still there after I was afraid I had miscarried.

V *is for my father's violin* and the cherished memory of his pulling it out every Christmas and standing behind me while I played carols at the grand piano. I come from a family of singers. My father would tap my head with the bow every time I hit a wrong note. These group sings taught me that no matter what, keep the rhythm going. I still play a lot of wrong notes, but I will never miss a beat!

W *is for the red wagon,* full of picture books and Matthew, my first baby. Every few days, we would head downtown to our little stone library to pick out a new batch of books.

X *is for the occasional X-rays* of my foot, just to make sure the needle that I stepped on fifty years ago, is still there, encapsulated in tissue, just as the doctor predicted. He had been unable to extract it, even with the help of a large magnet used for war wounds. The danger was that it would let loose one day, head straight for my heart and kill me instantly. He must have been right. I'm not dead yet.

Y *is for yodeling,* which seemed to come easily to me. I always had a low singing voice, but lurking behind the scenes was a mad soprano. I used to sing both Mary Martin and Ezio Pinza's parts of Some Enchanted Evening.

Z *is not for zebra.* It is for zoning (see Bankruptcy). We had been assured that the acre and a half zoning would allow us to subdivide the six acre parcel into three lots. We planned to sell off the mansion and own the two remaining seaside lots. It was a no-brainer, as the real estate hot shots used to say. This would be our last real estate venture. We would pay off all our other real estate debt and be set for the rest of our lives. It turned out to be a private way, which meant all the wealthy neighbors hired lawyers and that was that. My tearful call to the head of the zoning board of appeals saying that we would be ruined, had no effect. We lost everything. No wait, that's not true. We lost our possessions but learned something way more valuable. We are not our possessions.

lost and found

I long to be submerged,
engulfed by some thought or project
of music or paint or words.
Just take me,
pull me under
and drown me.
There will always be the fear of failure,
of not being deep enough
perceptive enough,
funny enough,
beautiful enough.
All true.
All I can do is bring my whole self to the thing,
everything I know,
crammed into a brain
that is starting to leak.
Is there enough left?
When I'm submerged I don't care.
I'm just happy to be lost.

cape cod

For two weeks every year
I became a Cape Cod explorer —
a suburban child allowed to wander
with heat rising, summer in full swing,
the morning sun splaying on the white clapboards,
salt air, soft grass, still wet with night,
the driveway spread with crushed clamshells
beginning their slow warming.
I walk on the still cool road to the sleepy corner store
to buy my father his newpaper, feeling
the world through my barefeet.
Wet grass, crushed shells, the strip of sand lining the road,
then onto the walkway of cool macadam
embedded with large stones,
just beginning to feel the heat.

what's my line?

To the nuns at the top of the hill,
I am a kind, gentle wise soul.
To my counterpoint teacher and classmates,
I am an older student with an interest in music.
To the woman who emailed me from France,
I am a sublime interpreter of Jacques Brel.
To the person who bought my painting of cows,
I am an artist who lives in the country.
To the custodial staff at the museum where my
husband works,
I am a high-brow, high-class woman.
To the businessman who invested in my singing career,
I am a flake.
To the townspeople who thought my ex-husband was a martyr
and a saint,
I was an impulsive, selfish woman.
I am still any of those people on any given day.

a trip in 5/4 time

I'm going to sail far out into the sea
I'm going to drift where no one else has gone
The birds will swim above my head and the fish
            will fly beneath me,
and I shall float and sing a liquid song

I'm going to climb way up into the snows
I'll be above where any tree can grow
The air will sing a violent song and try to steal the day
and I will hear the wail upon the wind

I'm going to walk upon the desert sands
to white expanses as of yet unknown
and mighty lizards come to me and tell of green oasis
where I can feel and drink what they can see

distant nearness

MOTHER PICKED UP A SALTSHAKER to make a toast — one of the first outward signs of her dementia. I began a series of regular visits. She would sit in the wing chair in the den, with her customary little glass of white wine and a small bowl of popcorn, looking out the sliding glass door at the trees blowing in the wind, remembering…tentatively, at first, those early days in Meriden when she was eight and her mother would cry if she didn't get a letter from one of her brothers or sisters back in Cleveland. She remembered the dumbwaiter in the house her father had found for them in Meriden, after his company transferred him there. The kitchen was in the basement. Her mother cried about that too.

She remembered watching the church hall dances out the second story window of that house on Orient St. and talked about my father deciding to set his sights on the Sheffield School of Engineering at Yale because of a kid in the neighborhood who was a student there. His only role model until then had been his immigrant father who was a streetcar driver in New Haven. Ma remembered the loveseats they bought as newlyweds. They were all the rage, she laughed. She later had them joined into what became the family couch — the sanctuary where we napped, read, watched TV, threw up; the couch where we would lie feverish, sipping ginger ale, waiting for Dr. Rutherford to pull his big black Cadillac up in front of the house and walk up the flagstone steps with his soft, leather black bag, full of penicillin.

Mother was not a sentimentalist. At first, she thought it was silly to sit and reminisce, but the notion grew on her as she remembered the old GE refrigerator with the big round, whirring motor sitting on top of it like a giant hat box or the day their new neighbors in Meriden called her father outside to look at the smoke coming out of the chimney. "You may burn soft coal in Cleveland, but we don't allow it here." Her father went inside and quickly ordered a load of Connecticut hard coal. Mother was astonished at all the stories still inside her head; that my father proposed to her as she lay on the sidewalk, thrown from his overturned Pontiac, that she skipped two grades in grammar school because her mother didn't think the teachers were smart enough, that her mother quoted Shakespeare and as an 80-year-old substitute teacher challenged the high school English class to start any line of Hamlet and she would finish it. The kids figured they were going to get away with murder, but instead filed out of class in a Shakespeare-induced trance.

With each wingchair chat, the past became clearer and more interesting than yesterday, the memories washing over her in rushes of distant nearness.

fugues and canons

I dream of grand solutions in my sleep,
of children's choruses overlapping with the violins,
of brilliant little fugues and canons,
of bold abstract landscapes
and tight short stories with surprising plots,
poetry with startling metaphors,
everything clear in the inkiness
of my brilliant brain.
But daylight dashes
all the notes against the picture window
and makes the paint slip down the table into dull grays.
Words stick to the pot
like overcooked oatmeal.
I am brilliant when I am asleep.
Chi flows.
I flourish in the lush vegetation
and swim in the vernal-est of pools,
pausing only to soak in the sun on hot flat rocks.
My mind crackles with one brilliant idea after another,
solving every conundrum.
But later, in the light of day,
I leave spoons in the garbage disposal
and forget my dentist appointment.

envy

The old woman says desire is like a poison. It can destroy
what is beautiful. Desire to have, to be, to want something
else. Something other. Contentment is the lack of longing.
Longing will make us unkind.
We measure who is richer, kinder, friendlier,
more popular, prettier, wittier.
Let's just be. Let's exist. But what
to do with ambition? curiosity?
striving? If only you would sell
me the contents of your pockets,
I could be happy. Your
belongings are things
I have not acquired.
If you acquired
them, they must be
valuable. If I do
not have them, I
must lack value.
The contented
old woman
smiles and
turns her
pockets
inside
out.
They
are
empty.

dazzled

THE EVENING IS PERFECT. The air, velvety. People strolling
in all directions, full of joy just to be alive and in this place.
And me, floating through the crowd as though in a dream,
a sea of twinkling lights leading me towards nothing but
another sea of twinkling lights. I drift in the direction of the
distant sound of music. A mariachi band! I enter a grand hall
glowing in lantern light, unfamiliar smells of exotic foods
hang in the air. Joyous diners, drinkers and dancers fill the

crowded expanse, skirts swirling in raucous intersecting Venn diagrams of brilliant reds and oranges. Transported. I have entered a place I did not know I missed. The push and pull of the night air echoes in the bellows of an accordionist.

La Vie en Rose. Under Paris Skies.

I am dazzled and wonder why I didn't choose this life! I was meant for a larger stage; more worldly, more alive! Spanish and now French voices and there, in the distance, German? Russian? The languages float in the soft night sky, lit only by the diffuse lantern light lining the cobblestone alleyway. I want to walk these crowded, happy streets forever. I want to speak the French I learned in college, try out my high school Spanish, my smatterings of German. I was meant to travel, to be a citizen of this wondrous world, in all its brutal enticements! I say yes to a small glass of wine that is offered to me. *Mais oui, monsieur! Mucho gusto*, he responds with a small bow and a smile. I continue walking, clutching my little souvenir wine glass as a token remembrance of this night. The time has come. It is past time to return. I walk slowly, drinking in the cool of the night, savoring the lightness of my being, the joy, now mixing with sorrow at a lost world. Am I chewing over choices made, unfulfilled dreams, wallowing in the spectre of Lost Opportunities?

But I love my life!

I make my way to the platform. The doors of the transport open silently. I enter the sleek white train in silence. We whoosh away from the lights, the laughter, the mad ecstasy.

Two stops and I am back at the hotel. My dear husband and three of my children (we had left the baby back home with a neighbor) are still playing and laughing in the pool. I had told them all I just wanted to zip over to see Epcot but would be back shortly. Happily splashing in the shallow end, they wonder what took me so long.

thinking about john updike

I do not really like poetry as much as I say I do.
I have never gone for the old fashioned flowery stuff
or the deliberately enigmatic runes
the teacher explains with patience,
but when I sat down in the sun this morning on my couch by
the east window,
looking out at the frozen river,
I could feel it.
I could feel the peace that accompanies
finding the exact words
to describe that glorious day
on the beach in Bermuda,
what I was thinking when I saw Whistler's Mother
at the Musée d'Orsée,
why it was that the smell of lavender
cheered me up that day,
I take the time to examine.
This morning, I sit in Borders Bookstore, reading
John Updike's poetic account of
his struggle with old age, loneliness
and death,
killing time while my computer
gets a brain transplant at the Apple Store,
which is full of youth,
bustling about in their techno bravado,
tapping on bright screens,
earbuds hanging.
I fit somewhere between John's lonely diagnosis of cancer
in an upper floor at Mass General
and the five-year-old boy who sits at a computer,

fur flaps of his baby hunting hat dangling,
playing computer games while waiting for his mother.
 don't seem to be rushing through life
I am Buddha
sitting on my couch in the sun

lucky

I don't know how to write love poetry
with limpid pools and roses, red
similes and metaphors carefully constructed
into a house of adoration.
I prefer to mention the way you wait for me
in the mud room
while I make sure I have all the layers
I need for our walk.
I prefer to think of how we fit
when I lie face down and you lie on top
of me
like a giant panda.

piano lessons

DO YOU REMEMBER how I was telling you about my teacher? Mrs. Haley was an old lady with white hair, glasses on a string, a Boston Terrier named Jerry and a house that smelled of old upholstery and stale coffee. Just the smell walking in used make my heart sink. That, and knowing that I hadn't practiced. The most I could hope for was that Jerry's ball would get lost under the credenza again, and he wouldn't stop yapping until somebody dug under there with a yard stick to fetch the ball.

Of course, old Mrs. Haley couldn't get down on her hands and knees herself, so she was always so happy that I was there to help. I would crouch down, acting as though the ball was hard to find, my face twisted up towards Mrs Haley so she'd be sure to know how hard I was trying. Finally, figuring enough was enough, I'd flick the ball out for the little mutt. Another good interruption was giving Mrs. Haley the check for the lessons. That was only once a month, but it usually made for a nice delay while Mrs. Haley rhapsodized about how wonderful my mother was and how prompt she was with her payment. I loved it when Mrs. Haley rhapsodized. You knew you were in for a good five to eight minutes, especially when she got going on The Eastern Star, which obviously was some kind of a club for older piano-teacher ladies. They would have Functions, where all the ladies dressed up and talked about how nice it was to be in The Eastern Star. Mrs. Haley used to play the piano at these Functions, or so she said, but this always surprised me because I could never picture Mrs. Haley actually playing the piano. I could only picture her talking about playing the piano.

Sometimes, she'd try to show me how to get emotion by holding my elbows and making them go 'round and 'round while I tried to play Für Elise at the same time. The only thing that did was to make me play all the wrong notes, but she would get a little annoyed, saying the notes weren't what mattered at that moment. I kind of wished they didn't seem to matter so much all the other times. And every other lesson or so, she'd lean over me to turn a page and I'd be forced to look at her flabby arms. I don't know why she didn't wear outfits with long sleeves so she wouldn't have to worry about all that flab. She would stop sometimes and wiggle her arms and say how gross they were. The other thing Mrs. Haley would do is take my hand in hers, which was kind of disgusting to begin with, and press her crooked, fat, sausagey fingers with thick, yellow, ridged fingernails, onto the back of my hand to show how much pressure to put on the keys. I was never really thinking about the piano at those moments. I just wanted her to let go of me so I could finish the lesson and get outside for some fresh air.

surrender

Writing, dreaming, skating through the unconscious
frozen field of shimmery waves
break the surface occasionally
lungs full of salt air
Float
unknown underwater currents
Surrender
Your thoughts are not your own.
They are larger than you
released to unlimited realms
in nightly trance.
Ah, to become more unconscious,
to allow neurons to explode in all directions
Abundance. Expansion.
I am the jailer and keeper of the keys.
I'll make a deal with myself, an auto-bribe,
to release me for short spurts
during waking hours,
to squeeze knowledge from a resistant, finite brain,
to abandon myself to another voice,
a disembodied, out of control voice,
capable of speaking foreign, unrecognizable tongues.

white night

Snow, stones
cold night
crisp and beautiful
still.
Walk with me on country roads
while snow falls.
Tonight's is a soft snow,
not the hurry up, wind-driven kind
a strolling, soft, warm snow.
Flakes gather quickly on hats, scarves, eyebrows, shoulders
but it's not too much this night.
Let's walk forever.
The world should always be this white,
this quiet,
this black,
this peaceful,
this slow.
Ancient stone walls line the road,
reminders that we are not the first here.
We take our places in the line of other lovers of these woods.
Long, time-packed roads,
leading only from one lone house to another.
White clapboard breaks on the long, dark road.
Anechoic snow, muffling the sound of our shuffling.
Cold night
      crisp and beautiful
           still.

swimming

ONCE A YEAR the girl goes to Boston on the train with her mother to buy her school uniform. They sit on the cracked leather seats, thinking their own thoughts. Dressed in her Sunday best, the girl looks out through the clouded windows at a universe much larger and more complex than the one she knows, so much more than her house, her walk to school, the pond where she swims in the summer, her neighborhood with its neat and tidy houses. She sees huge, square brick buildings with windows as big as cars, dirty little stores with magazine racks out front, different-looking people, walking streets of different widths. She wonders what her life would be like if she had been born in a different place. As the train passes within a few feet of a building with a wall of glass, she sees the crystal blue of the water and the white reflections dancing on the walls and ceilings, a woman swimming laps. The woman lifts her head to look. The train slows for the next stop. The girl leans forward in her seat, her face pressed to the window, twisting, twisting, wondering what her life would be like in that pool. She stands up to get off the train, telling her mother she needs a larger life than her mother is able to provide. The door opens and she jumps to her freedom, watching her mother's face in the train window. *I would never be able to find the right words to explain. I want to dive into that pool and spread my arms wide, feel the pull of the water against my skin. Am too late to choose a life other than this one? to know the opposite of what I know?*

The train disappears into a tunnel.

THE WOMAN IS SWIMMING LAPS in the neighborhood when she hears the train. Her daughters are sitting on the edge of the pool. The woman lifts her head to watch the train go by and sees a young girl peering out the window. She stops swimming and thinks *who was I when I was her age? What was I thinking? Who was I listening to? Why did I listen? Have I truly chosen this pool I'm in? What might I have been if I had been fully alive back then? I followed in the footsteps of my mother and my older sisters — marriage, babies, kindness and neighborhood parties!* The daughters stop swishing their legs in the water, look at each other, then back at their mother, who gets out of the pool. *I'll be back as soon as I can.* She wraps a towel around her waist, walks out of the building and runs down the sidewalk, her goggles still on her head. She hops on the train just as it is pulling away, finds a seat next to an old Chinese man with a bag full of empty bottles. He smiles and gives a small bow with his head. She bows in return, her goggles looking at him. The two sit primly, the Chinese man and the towel-wrapped woman, looking straight ahead. Are they thinking about one another? Is she wondering why he collects empty soda cans and is he wondering why she is in her bathing suit? The Chinese man turns to her and says, The mind is a strange and funny thing. In the summer it longs for winter, and in the winter, it longs for summer. He gathers up his bottles and gets off at the next stop. She follows him.

✳

THE OLD LADY WATCHES out her back door, her mind empty of thought. She opens the door and walks in the direction of the setting sun, not knowing where she is headed or why. She heads straight, through the back yard, between the gap in the rhododendrons and into the woods. Remember how Grandma used to quote Shakespeare? Nobody memorizes things anymore. Raspberries! Watch out for the prickers! Let's go swimming at Morse's Pond like we used to. Did you remember your boots, honey? Don't forget to call when you get there. Straight across Emerson Road, by the black pond, across the highway and down into the gulley she goes. Have you finished your homework? Daddy, can I come too? Out of the gulley and up the next hill. Can I make it? Yes. Where will I go? Straight ahead. Across the highway. What if I get cold? Am I hungry? It doesn't matter. The trees are so pretty, don't you think, dear? With all that snow? They look like people. Oh! The Christmas lights! The lights are pretty, aren't they, dear? Do you like the white ones or the colored ones? Where shall I go? What do you mean? Over this fence, it's not too high. I can make it. Maybe we can go swimming! Front yards. Back yards. Stay in the backyard, sweetheart. I don't want you to get lost. Step high, darling, over the brambles. We're almost there.

in praise of flounder

Checkered tablecloths and checkered curtains
take me to a table by the sea.
I'll sit with the warm sea breeze
at my back and a glass of wine
at my lips,
to toast the tides
to praise the flounder for their cleverness
to stay on into night and watch the phosphorescence
dance from wave to wave,
thinking *what magic!*
how much larger than the world is the sea!

the sea

The sky is so deep, blue beyond possibility
today, much brighter than the ocean.
The blues of the water and the sky meet every day
in stunning demonstrations of the laws of probability.
Singing Beach, a half mile stretch of heaven,
my playground as a young mother,
idyllic days of laughter, heat and water, light and air,
sun and sea.
I stride from one end to the other,
superstitiously touching the rocks at either end.
Did I understand the gift back then?
I thought I did, but
thinking now that perhaps I didn't.
Fully.
Impossible when you have.
You need to have, then not have, to truly understand.
Now when I get a chance to walk the length of a beach,
it is with ecstasy.
I can hardly contain my spirit in my body.
One long ago October, I walked West Beach
on a brilliant left-over summer day.
At the deserted far end I took off all my clothes
and made love to the sea and to myself.
At that moment, I knew, really knew
that I was enchanted.

the all-together

We sat on the hot sands of a beach
a few miles north of South Beach,
wearing only our hats
both so thankful for the internet,
without which we would have
spun through parallel never-intersecting orbits,
never to have shared cautious information
about our children and our past loves,
never to have ended up on this beach,
watching an excited group of similarly naked people
gathering around a sea turtle
washed up on the shore.
I wanted to take a picture,
but you frowned on the idea,
and even though we'd been together
only a few months,
it felt like we had known each other forever,
and I put my camera back in my bag,
knowing you were right.

salvation

When I tire of the modern world
and all its glamor
and when I grow weary
(women do get weary
wearing the same shabby dress),
I go to the local Salvation Army Store
to pick out a few new things.
The stuff there
marches to a different beat.
Madison Avenue may be showing only
blousy tops and short-shorts this season
but The Salvation Army has it all —
sling-backs, patent leather spectators,
Christmas sweater vests, felt hats with feathers,
lined trench coats like your father's
(maybe it *is* your father's).
I thumb through all the clothing,
thinking of the lives that have been lived.
Was this a favorite jacket?
Were these shoes dyed maroon
to match a bridesmaid's dress?
Sad closets-full of a husband's clothes,
hand-painted teacups from an Italian aunt.
The things that I have worn will sift through
the hands of my kids,
onto a rented fold-up table in the driveway,
where the neighbors will pick and choose.
The rest will end up here,
sorted by category and color
at The Salvation Army Store.

there but for the grace of god

THE PHONE RINGS and you don't know if it's the phone or the new, beeping pill dispenser your husband bought so he could leave you alone in the house for long stretches of time. Before that, you were in charge of knowing which gaily colored pill was which and when to take the Rasagiline, or the Levodopa, the Azilect, the Sinemet or the anti-depressant, hoping the color-coded remedies might stop the slow and steady march of Parkinson's Disease.

From the outside, I am helpless. I don't know how you keep it all straight. If only yours was the variation of Parkinson's that only affects coordination and causes the tremors.

That would have been a gift compared with what you got — a version that causes the relentless creep of dementia, like the hot lava flow that devours entire villages in the horror movies. You are slowly losing your mind, clinging to your grip on the day-to-day, but mostly reverting to what has come before in your life, grasping at memories of our growing-up years like they were yesterday, imagining that the eight of us are all crowded into the old Pontiac *woody* station wagon to go to the drive-in, or that our youngest brother Michael is still alive, or that we still live in the old house on Thackeray Road, or that Mother and Dad are in the next room.

They are not.

But there are others too, you tell me. There's a baby sleeping in a crib, who needs its diapers changed. There's a little boy standing in your driveway, or a bunch of teenagers goofing off in the backyard. You are constantly seeing the babies and children you were never able to have, the only one of the six of us who was unable to conceive, a particularly tough dose in a baby-centric family. You were a Latin teacher, a grammarian, a meticulous explainer of the ablative absolute or the anomalies of the fifth declension or the use of the vocative case.

So now, your telephone chat has become a strange invention of half-sentences and invented words, all with the correct, assured tone of the salesman and the etymological know-how of the Latin teacher. *It would be...grubble stang and so forth...so interesting, for instance...if the house weren't...sub rosa...it's only two doors down, but it's the same...conglomeration.*

And why should we be surprised when, before you can go out for a little walk, you decide to line up all your jewelry on the bed, to take inventory, to consider which pair of large

sterling silver earrings you might choose to match the wilted black fleece sweatsuit you now wear every day, while the bright quilted jackets, elegant slips of silk blouses and tasteful black slacks lie fallow in your closet.

And the pills keep changing, this one, combatting the decline of motor function; that one, batting back dementia; a Hobson's choice between two distasteful outcomes, as you sail haltingly between the Scylla and Charybdis of a turbulent disease. Funny, that on any given day, you still might remember those two treacherous cliffs described in Virgil's Aeneid, a treasure of knowledge shared by several of us in our classics-crazy household!

You were always the fancy one in the family. I envied your pink, flowery canopy bed and the delicate white secretary desk in the corner, where you wrote neatly in little notebooks, in a handwriting that was so elegant, people would ask you to do their wedding invitations. I was only four years younger than you and was probably in line for the canopy and the desk, but the world seemed to shift in those four years; from stockings, silk dresses and patent leather pocketbooks to torn jeans and bandanas.

Your stories and concerns are often filled now with paranoia and apprehensions, suspicions or fears of criticism. I try to untangle what is disease and what is part of your DNA, from our family that seemed full of laughter, happiness, and success, but which also hid a raw underbelly of competition, fear of failure and thin skin.

You are the canary-in-the-coal mine of the family now, laying bare all of our inner faults, the limitations and neuroses that the rest of us are still capable of disguising with the quick two-step of Irish wit.

life drawing
class

a room full of men with unused
pencils poised over
blank sheets of paper
waiting for the
model to untie her
blue silk kimono and let it
slide to the floor

house cleaning

I sit in the early morning stillness
with my third cup of coffee,
chasing ideas about love, about what makes us tick,
what compels us to act, why the world so dissatisfied,
but I am unable to land any single thought on the shore
and wonder if Thoreau sat on a flat rock by the pond,
trying to think up something new to say about the
sunrise or the carpet of forest lilies so fragrant in the early
morning, but instead couldn't stop thinking about when to
bring his dirty laundry over to his mother's place.

why i'm thinking of taking up whittling

I went to a poetry reading last night
thinking I wanted to be a poet —
to publish little booklets full of hard-won truths,
to labor at night under a small lamp in the kitchen,
describing the feelings I had
when I lost my virginity
or when my first child went to kindergarten;
but the intentional nature of it all
in that art gallery full of unsellable art,
the wringing out of words,
the self-satisfied lingering on hard-won word combinations
with practiced modulation and hand gestures
the benevolent dispensing of wisdom,
the self satisfied air in the room
threatening at any moment
to extinguish the patchouli-scented candles,
made me slip out the door between poet number two
and the guitar-playing poet who was
about to take the microphone.

ironing in the cellar

MY MOTHER used to spend a lot of time in the cellar. With
The Mangle — a machine the size of a small car that looked
like an organ console without the keyboard. It was the marvel
ironing machine of the '40s and '50s which allowed house-
wives to do *all the ironing right at home!*

On the other side of the cellar, my father spent Sundays
listening to *Live at the Met*, even though he knew nothing
about opera. During particularly dramatic arias, he would
give the play-by-play. "Oh...oh, he's gonna get her. No...wait...
she's getting away..." while he dictated weekly
sales reports into his Grey Autograph Machine, a magical
dictaphone contraption that etched his voice in concentric
circles onto filmy blue disks. My father sold electroplating
equipment and supplies. Whenever dad sold an *Automatic*, he
was happy and life in our house was calm.

An *Automatic* was a huge vat that coated any object with
chrome, silver or gold; car bumpers, picture frames, refrigera-
tor handles and probably an occasional gangster.

My mother never went to the cellar on the weekends. She
tried to stay away from dad when he was working down there.
We all did. We never knew when he would, when egged on
by either a sub-par sales week or a crappy opera, ascend the
cellar stairs loaded for bear, attacking any one of us who was
stupid enough to be within reach of his sarcastic anger about
what a mess the house was.

But back to Mother's Mangle. It had a red on-off toggle switch
and a five-foot padded roller which was controlled by knee-oper-
ated levers, leaving the hands free to feed it with wrinkled sheets,
pillowcases, tablecloths. Mother would catch the item on the
back side, fold it in half and send it through again. Over and over.

She spent a lot of time in the dimly lit cellar, with a sheet of white and gold-speckled linoleum the only thing that protected her from the frigid concrete floor. She loved it down there with her Mangle and her thoughts, a Bel-air menthol cigarette burning nearby. It was the only place in the house where she could be alone, the six of us running around upstairs like banshees.

Every Christmas, mother would send me down to the back corner of the cellar, near the boiler, to spray toxic gold spray on everything she could think of; pinecones, wreaths, nativity scenes. (She probably could have used an Automatic.) I felt like the chosen one. I can still hear the rattle of the beads inside the spray can and smell the thrill of those intoxicating Holiday Fumes.

But this is not about me or dad, it's about my mother and her Mangle. Steam, press, roll, fold. She was a master. Ironing my father's shirts was an artform. Spray starch, collar inserted first, lower roller, steam, raise roller, cuffs, lower roller, steam, raise roller. The body of the shirt was the last to run the gauntlet. Mother hung the shirts on a wobbly rack. At the end of the session, she would stub out her Belair and bring the shirts up to my dad's closet, two floors up, being careful not to step on our Tiddly Winks, spread around on the oriental rug in the front hall.

I used to wonder if the Mangle was named after my older brother. The story goes that one day, when he was very little, he figured out how to turn on the red switch and work the levers. There were no table-cloths around, so he put in his hand and lowered the roller.

Until that day, none of us was aware that you could take skin from one part of the body and graft it onto a different part.

the pilgrimage

THEY HAD ARRANGED TO MEET IN THE MOUNTAINS;
the daughter, doing a year of teaching in England, the mother,
alone in a little Boston city apartment trying to figure out
life after divorce. The blue convertible, the little stucco house
in the Pyrenees with a view of Mount Canigou, the sangrias
on the road to Collioure, the empty solemnity of Barcelona
on Good Friday, sunshine gleaming off the Gaudi tiles, the
outdoor café on Easter morning in the little town of Céret, a
statue of Christ, carried through the winding streets; none of
it could fully clear the air.

half light

I TURN OUT THE LIGHTS and step on to the side porch, just to feel the air, cool finally, after the heat has knocked the life out of us. But now we can breathe again. The night air is alive, a breeze coming up through the neighborhood from the water. I can smell the sea or am I tasting it? the clam flats, the lines of sea lettuce left by the high tide, a long curly shawl of kelp wrapped around me in an old black and white photo of my childhood, as though I'm headed to the opera, the slime of seaweed trapped inside my bathing suit.

There must be more than the five senses that Aristotle granted us, overlapping in unexpected ways; the taste of the sea, the salt, the healing of it, the glow of my father's cigarette in the dark evening screened-in porch, the earth smell of the lake, the head-spinning euphoria of love at seventeen, the sight of my newborns covered in afterbirth, followed years later by the bumping up against containment. I couldn't name the taste of it enough to explain to myself why I had to leave. I could only smell the premature death. I can still touch the euphoria of freedom entwined with the twisting guilt of the exit and now swallows gather and swirl in the fading half-light of evening while our little lives flow on, perhaps re-incarnated from other ages, other beings. These, and other exuberant thoughts, were forbidden in my childish church-bound days. But now, everyone is wrong and everyone is right and I suppose I should feel lost but instead I feel like the swallows, gathering, gathering to leave this place in wanderlust, longing to go, to travel, to see, to tell the stories while time is passing and yet the sea will rise and fall like it always has, even when I am no longer standing on my side porch thinking about it. I could swim in a warm, wavy sea and never turn back, ride the swells, thinking about nothing and everything, like is there a God and what does it matter really, although my aunt Joan was certain because when I asked *Who is God?* (she *was* a former nun after all), we stood under a gigantic beech tree whose limbs stretched wide like giant arms. *Love*, she answered, without skipping a beat. *Love.*

OK. I get that.

New moon tonight.

the lady who lives within walking distance

EVERY DAY, on the sidewalk in front of my house, the lady floats past my window, erect, her head held high; not shuffling or plodding along like the others. She wears fine, thin leather oxfords with tie-up laces, her delicate face framed by snow-white hair gathered into a French twist. With the bearing of a Roman goddess, she floats by my front window with her head held high, hair as white as moonflowers. She sometimes turns her head to admire my little sidewalk garden, scattered with rocks I have collected from treasured beaches. Perhaps she spent lazy summers as a child on the coast of Maine, building teetering towers of small striped or volcanic rocks, coal black and shiny. Perhaps she had considered heading off to medical school, maybe to study Jung, a country girl with hairpins holding up the twist of her ebony hair, now white as delphiniums, her head held high, floating, floating…

Or perhaps she became a professor, say, of Medieval English or no, maybe the surrealist French poets, drifting from Rimbaud to Baudelaire, eventually receiving an honorary degree from the Sorbonne. And for the award ceremony, I imagine she wore a rose-colored sari she had received from a former lover back in her younger student days in Mumbai.

But now, after it all, her hair, white as cherry blossoms, she is content to float by on the sidewalk in front of my house.

on the taunton

this morning,
just before dawn,
a narrow sliver of a moon,
pale as baby's flesh
hangs over our frozen river.
Hiroshige must have lived here
we sit at our breakfast table
every morning, candles lit,
looking out to the rosy dawn edges
of an indigo sky
you, who have for many years,
contemplated the planets
with all their frivolous paths
and baffling wonder,
have brought the moon to me.
why wonder
if I would have found it on my own.

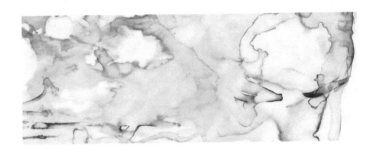

black ice

THE MORNING IS HEAVY with the sweet smell of the linden tree. The gentle white-haired lady who walks by my porch every day, stops to say she was in a car accident and now finds out her car has been declared a total loss. She purses her lips, trying to hold back tears as she presses her fist against her solar plexus. But wait, there's more. Her daughter was fired yesterday. The parks department is being disbanded. The DPW will take it over. "The DPW?" she scoffs in disgust, pressing her delicate, balled-up hand against her ribs again. I tell her I will pray for her even though I'm not exactly sure what that means. Our grandchildren are growing taller, disappearing into their worlds, leaving cherished traces of history. We teach them how to play cribbage. The lady asks if I am familiar with astrology. "Saturn Return," she says, "is particularly bad for my birth sign." On another day, she told me she had studied Jung with Joseph Campbell in the early 60s. Wouldn't it be lovely to have another go-'round, to sit in that classroom, to drink in the persona, the anima, the shadow, the self, the stars, the moon, the all of it. Saturn is a planet of rules, restrictions, and responsibilities. Time, patience, maturity, karma and hard work.

The planets teach life lessons, want us to take things slow. Saturn Return happens every 29.5 years. I'll be dead next time.

Drink in the wood stoves and the school plays, the envy and striving, the real estate deals and bankruptcy, the divorce, my one-woman theater plays and risky ventures, the love and sex, the secret yearnings and the macaroni and cheese. Other years, past lives are racing, racing towards the future. The thrill of Christmas Eve, the birthing of babies, the BeeGees, Midsummer Night's Dream in Regent's Park, the blueberry pancakes, the warm waves at Horseneck Beach, the old fisherman with the long, aluminum pole, stabbing in circles through the hole in the ice, feeling for the black eels wiggling in the dark mud, the train to Avignon; all, part of the tapestry. Jung's ancestral memories, not obvious to the eye, describe a merging of the conscious and the unconscious.

From the full moon in July to the full moon in August, the world is ruled by greenhead flies. Queen Anne's lace swims white in the meadow. The chaplain sits by my aunt's bedside for prayer, wants to know if she would like to receive The Anointing of the Sick, which used to be called The Last Rites, which used to be called Extreme Unction. The oil at the end. Sounds like a fine idea.

On another day, in another layer, we sit in the theater. The storyteller sweeps us up into his old neighborhood, tells of growing up with sisters, serving cheese and crackers at their parents' cocktail parties, of intending to borrow a quart of milk from the neighbor but staying instead for blueberry pancakes, of the doc who parked his car in the old garage with the green tin roof and the girl who lived in the alley, the one who thought she was dumb but got a scholarship and how he thought she was so beautiful. When he finally got up the courage to kiss her, she smiled and said, "It's about time" and how later she died of a heart that suddenly stopped. The storyteller closes with the dark magic of skating on black ice, with the stars and the moon.

Skating, skating, on and on into the night.

aunt joan

My aunt is disappearing
along with all the small talk, the old stories
the laughs… Sometimes,
when I visit
her eyes flash for an instant
with an old light,
before she disappears again into the mist.
She still has a phone, still knows how to push the big button
marked KATE. She doesn't call much anymore, but
sometimes, at odd hours, she will call and clear as a bell,
say she loves me and call me *kiddo* like the old days.
But mostly she can't hear me. She's forgotten her hearing aids.
Again.
I say I love her.
She hears that and answers,
"I know. We are so lucky to have each other."
But more often than not, she can't hear me.
In these moments, she is pouring out beautiful messages
of love and devotion and pray for me,
I need your prayers
but she can't hear any of my responses.
She grumbles, "I can't hear you"
but also "anyway, I love you, kiddo" -
godlike expressions of love,
unreturnable,
like the mysterious no-man's land
between this life and the next -
between us, the still-living and our beloveds
who have gone before.

We tell them we love them and
what would we be without them.
They are answering us
but we can't hear them,
through that thin veil
of there and here.

music in the air

The first requisite of a good melodic line is a
sense of direction.

Paper doves float with intention, in ever-rising undulations
from the nave to the rafters of Salisbury Cathedral, the white
of the paper kaleidoscoping with the shifts of sun through
stained glass. The crowd gawks in admiration.

Music is the silence between the notes.

The full moon clears the horizon, slowly at first, then in a
faster than expected crescendo, exploding into a vivid orange,
followed by a long slow diminuendo as it rises into the sky,
draining itself white into a thin rising melodic line.

I stole everything I ever heard, but mostly
I stole from the horns.

A cluster chord of starlings rests on dark winter branches, then bursts forth in a blaze of horns, scattering from unison to four octaves in an instant.

In putting together two or more melodic lines to form
counterpoint, each line must be good in itself.

On the flats at low tide, a crowd of barnacled boulders plays a dirge, accompanied by multiple ripples of sand, curving in rapidly repeating parallel thirds.

I frequently hear music in the heart of noise.

The vacuum cleaner sings an E flat. The pulse of the blender cuts through the hum of the fluorescent lights. The blare of a fire engine's siren screams through the night its repeated, repeated, warnings in a tritone, banned in the Middle Ages for its unpleasant interval of three whole steps. They called it *The Devil's Interval.* Gershwin didn't know he wasn't supposed to use it. It became his signature.

The heart of music is its rhythm.

The pulsing whistle of the steam heat coming up, the clank, clank of the long run of hot water pipes from the third-floor condo to the basement, the quick tremolo of it being shut off, the C natural of electronic devices, the accelerando clack, clack, clack of a pebble embedded in your car tire.

Music is the divine way to tell beautiful,
poetic things to the heart.

In the dementia unit at the assisted living place, I land with gentle, but firm conviction on the last chord of *The Moonlight Sonata.* My aunt, who played the piano for 90 years, has slept through the whole thing. But perhaps not. She lifts her head and murmurs, "The water is lovely."

CREDITS: KENT KENNAN, CLAUDE DEBUSSY, ELLA FITZGERALD, KENNAN, GEORGE GERSHWIN, WINTON MARSALIS, PABLO CASALS

rubber soul

In a crowded green-line car at rush hour, we stand,
finding whatever handhold possible,
swaying with feet firmly planted, a mixture
of determination, laughter, loneliness or bravado.
A kid gets on at Kenmore with his boombox.
We steel ourselves for the assault of sound,
preparing for the worst. Then comes the
pleading, pleading, quietly through the car.
Is there anybody going to listen to my story
all about the girl who came to stay?
Our gazes soften,
the car lifts from the tracks and
floats past distant, abandoned stops,
all of us slowly, slowly drifting away.

waning moon

I step outside to get the morning paper
in the Chinese bathrobe
I had no right buying,
back when the kids were little and money
was much harder
to come by.

I can see my breath, blurry in the moist cold dark,
feels like snow about to come by, now
sledding down the hill in front of the old house
into the empty snow-packed street,
no cars come by back then,
in my Chinese bathrobe
the neighborhood still asleep,
except for the blurry television
and the few forgotten Christmas lights.
Come by back then, yes, come by.
Every year, my father rigged up a spotlight
to shine on the wreath on our front door,
red ribbon and gold-painted pinecones,
         year after year
long extension cord from the cellar,
in the dark air across the street,
the blurry television on so early
in the house where the young mother
is dying of ovarian cancer.
Awake in the moist cold,
wide awake,
her little children asleep upstairs,
through darkened windows,
the moist air filled with the blurry
hope of resurrection or reincarnation.
A church bell rings six times.
I stand there
longer than usual,
in my worn-out Chinese bathrobe
with the waning moon.
Then I turn
back into my warm house
to make coffee and read the morning paper.

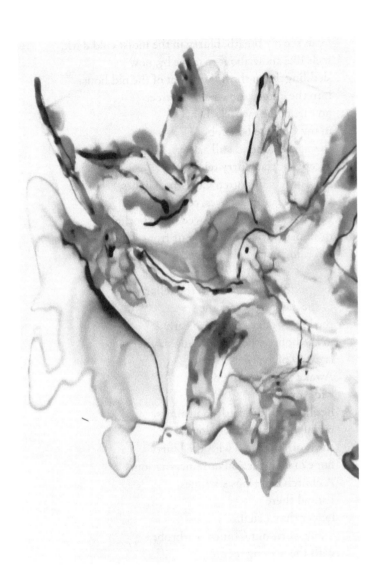

circular motion

ONE LONG-AGO GLORIOUS SUMMER, I commuted to my
waitressing job by motorboat and the world stretched out
to the horizon. Now old and sleepless, I take a bit of THC
and let my dreams wander in gyres from endless hours spent
with a boyfriend, riding to nowhere in his pea green Buick
LeSabre convertible, to performing my one-woman musical
drama to a sold-out crowd, to watching Rocky and Bullwin-
kle in utter loneliness while nursing my first baby. Perhaps
I shouldn't have gone for motorcycle rides with that violin
player. I roll over and think of our stately Dutch colonial
on a dead-end street and my dead-end basement apartment
where I desperately sought space and time to think, wonder-
ing if my center would hold. I drift from glorious swims in
cold mountain streams to long car rides where the intimate
anonymity allowed for confessions. With stolen glances,
we pass mile-markers and exit ramps, speaking of the past
in ways that were impossible face to face. Eyes on the road,
straining to see through a blizzard of vulnerabilities, we are
both soothed by the rhythm of the windshield wipers and
the green glow of the dashboard lights, even as old sorrows
seep in through the air vents. Did you open those letters that
were in my top dresser drawer? you know, the ones I burned
afterwards, sending pieces of charred paper circling, circling,
then drifting up the chimney on hot-air drafts? Everything up
in smoke with no sparks left behind. But mirabile dictu, love
re-appears and the dactyls and spondees of iambic pentameter
gallop along without my even having to write the sonnet.

tea with lemon

MARY LOU ARRIVES with a sweet little bouquet of tulips and grape hyacinths from her garden and settles into the large comfy chair in our little over-crowded living room. I ask her if she'd like some tea. She says decaffeinated and we rat-a-tat-tat back and forth about lemon tea or just a slice of lemon in water, and I wonder if I even have something decaffeinated that I could put lemon in, and she doesn't seem to really want just a slice of lemon in hot water, and because we are not as close with each other as we act, or maybe it's just that I'm getting too old to make any new, true friendships, I feel nervous and don't ask her to clarify. She has lived in this town for forty years and has boatloads of friends and if it weren't for the bankruptcy and the divorce, I could have stayed and kept some friends, but I tell myself I'm all the richer for the adventures I've had.

I bring her a mug of the only decaffeinated tea I have — a sleep-inducing brand called Bedtime and just hope she doesn't fall asleep in my comfy chair. I bring the tea and a few sugary cookies out on my favorite little faded yellow wooden tray — the one with the pink roses, that I bought at a yard sale around the corner a few years ago. The lady of the house was a new acquaintance but shortly after that yard sale, she dropped dead out of nowhere. So, it's either a lucky tray or an unlucky one. I never used to get nervous about having somebody over for a visit and wonder if it's the pandemic or if my former extraversion is just disappearing with advancing age. Mary Lou talks about how she's a bit stalled creatively these days and then adds with a laugh that she's sold five paintings during the pandemic. Wow, I say, that's great, thinking that my own paintings are too strange to sell, and why can't I just paint abstract fields of color that match people's upholstery and be done with it, instead of ostriches or zebras in bizarre landscapes, but doesn't everything come down to selling yourself and maybe I've just had it up to here with creativity. *Oh, you're so talented!* they always say, and I smile and nod and say things like, *Oh we all have gifts and talents*, which is true but they don't seem to know that one can be tormented by it all, but in general I'm pretty good at making lemonade out of lemons and besides, it just makes sense that some people seem to be able to sell their gifts better than others. Perhaps it's all about blogging and the funny thing is, I've always been a good schmoozer but maybe I'm just exhausted now at the thought of a sales pitch. But good for Mary Lou and I really do like her, so I feel small for feeling small and begin to wonder what's the matter with me and why, even though I'm good at so many things, I am driven to be good at everything the other person is good at. I suppose it comes down to being competitive, probably a result of … Mary Lou interrupts with, *Are these cookies gluten-free?*

i never lived in paris

I never ran for elective office
I never married a millionaire
I never lived in Paris
I never scored the winning goal
I never went to cooking school in Italy
I never belonged to a knitting group or a country club
I never dined at the Ritz
I never joined the convent
or receive a prize in a barbecue contest
but I did take my top off on the cross country
ski trail behind my house,
dine in a Boston restaurant with Eartha Kitt,
get a postcard from John Updike,
and a letter from Seamus Heaney,
sing with Claude Bolling in his cellar music room,
and hear my composition played in Carnegie Hall.

waterskiing

Some days there doesn't seem to be much to say.
I could write about a bird
or that the sun is setting later these days
or that I haven't visited my mother in too long
or that I worry about growing old
and I wish we had enough money to really fix up the barn
or that I don't see my children very much
because life spreads out more than it used to
but I couldn't have lived in one small,
stultifying town my whole life,
so I won't write about that.
Or I could have said it's Friday
and we'll make a pizza tonight
or I could have thought about the thrill of making
something up out of nothing
and how it's a miracle every time
and how Billy Collins is right,
that many people, instead of letting themselves loose to
waterski across the surface of a poem,
they want instead to
tie the poem to a chair with a rope and
torture a confession out of it.
Today feels a bit tortured.
I think I'll take a walk.

four-part invention

I TRIED TO WRITE AN AUTOBIOGRAPHY, which seemed a
bit overwhelming, to be perfectly frank. I thought about my
sister Geddy's anemia and how my grandmother gave her a
trip to Ireland to fatten her up, which morphed to a 21-day
whirlwind tour of European capitals for three of us; the Book
of Kells in Dublin, A Midsummer Night's Dream in Regents'

Park in London, The Louvre in Paris, and the frenchmen
who picked us up and brought us to the Bois de Bologne for
a picnic. That was where I learned the word for a *wasp* in
French when one of the guys drank wine out of the bottle
and screamed multiple times, *J'ai bu une guêpe! J'ai bu une
guêpe!* and the picture of me and my sisters in Rome, throwing
coins over our shoulders into the Trevi Fountain. I was 16. I
wonder what I wished back then. We wore matching dresses
that my mother had made, which made me think, wouldn't
it be interesting to write an autobiography centered around
articles of clothing you remember, like the fancy spectator
pumps I bought in high school that always hurt because they
were nine and a halfs instead of tens. I was embarrassed to
tell the salesman how big my feet were. Or the forest green
full length velveteen cape with a hood, lined with white satiny
looking material that I made for my junior prom. My sister
wore it later that year for her rainy February wedding.

But it was all too boring, so I decided to go to bed instead,
thinking how I had always wanted to write a nocturne simply
because I like the sound of the word; something at night,
perhaps a gentle lullaby to soothe the people, or maybe it had
more to do with the moonlit nocturnes of Whistler. Those
paintings are pure magic, come to think of it. But of course,
the trouble was I didn't know how to paint or write music or
play an instrument, but I discovered if I just let myself become
very still, I could snatch melodies from the air around me. I
could hear the notes floating, and dreamed of Carnegie Hall.

My neighbor Louisa had a grand piano sitting idly in her
big living room; a gift from her grandmother, who was a
concert pianist. Louisa is tone deaf. I figured if I could just sit
there on the piano bench, something would come to me, but it
never did. I did count the keys though. There are 88 of them,
some black and some white.

moon tide

SUMMER IS FLEEING. The microwave clock ticks in time with the sparrow's teacher-teacher-teacher, through the still open screen. I extricate my bicycle from the tangle of faded morning glory vines in the screen house and head for the beach, passing two old ladies talking about their favorite fall chicken dishes, a gray-haired woman pushing a grown child in a wheelchair. I ride on. A sudden burst of wind startles mask-wearing mourners at the town cemetery. Further out of town, a tractor kicks up dust in a field full of bulging pumpkins. The sweet-and-sour smell of manure mixes with the thick salt air. I ride along to the beach at the end of the road and lay my bike down to sit in the still warm sand. A lone swimmer slices through a glassy moon tide to the distant moaning of seals.

capuccino morning

PILGRIMS FLOCK to the new coffee shop in town, everything painted pure white, light fixtures hang from soaring ceilings, with upscale lamp shades fashioned from upturned willow baskets. Two women in comfy chairs lean in towards each other over croissants and cappuccinos, dishing dirt, sharing secret gripes...*I would never in a million years...the dog... expensive pillows...feathers everywhere...you guys good again?... oh yeah, I don't even know what was wrong...*

A lady walks by outside, stealing a sidelong glance of her flowing turquoise poncho reflection in the squeaky-clean floor to ceiling windows. A bowl of water for passing dogs. The bing of a text from my brother about his macular degeneration. Where did we fall apart? Was it money? Mother? Distant for several years, old age is now jostling us into forgiveness.

A lady walks by, red cloche on her head, corduroy biker jacket, with *Heartbreaker* written in sequins over a heart shaped doily design.

I hear Portuguese, and a sneeze. Gray skies, rain coming, what do we all do to fill our time, earn a buck, find belonging? A dog stops and raises a paw, looking for a reward.

Dogs begging, doors squeaking, earth spinning.

Over the backbeat of the house music and the murmurs of customers, I open my book and read of the 17th century sin-eaters who were paid sixpence to absorb the sins of the dead ones, then fed with a bowl of beer and a bite from the loaf of bread set on the chest of the corpse. Small change for lugging all those sins through life.

I sip my latte, careful to spare the heart-shaped foam.

the fish monger

AT THE FISH COUNTER of our local grocery store, the seafood is arranged in orderly rows, receding towards the back of the case, appearing to shrink and disappear as planes converge into distant vanishing points. A friend is eyeing the salmon. She is soft-spoken and kind, petite and orderly, her blond hair, cut in a tidy bowl shape. A dancer and a painter, she creates peaceful pastel landscapes with softened edges, gracious ballerinas, twisting towards perfection and rusted tractors in peaceful, overgrown fields. She has also illustrated many children's books with kind old-fashioned shopkeepers or hedgehogs or donkeys, who all go about their business with patience and time-honored integrity.

As we consider which fish to buy, I ask the usual *How are things?* She hesitates, looking up towards Today's Specials and says, *Well, we've hit a bit of a hitch in the road.*

Fauvist greens and crimsons seep through the cracks, tilting the usual towards the strange and radical. *I have been diagnosed with stage 4 metastatic breast cancer,* she tells me. She is speaking a foreign language. *It has spread to my bones.*

The fish monger is now a flat cartoon, broken into triangles, outlined in black. The pickerel flatten, their glassy eyes popping from their silver skins. The monkfish begin to swim out of their prison, flapping up towards the ceiling fan, where they fragment and shatter into a million pieces. Squid foreshorten into twisting ballerinas, salmon steaks distort into old tractors, appearing shallower than the original and the grocery aisles skew off in a dizzying display of multiple perspectives.

I don't remember if I bought any fish.

no time to be timid

LUXURIATING IN MY MORNING SHOWER, everything is crystal clear. I know where I'm going. I understand everyone's lives. I am pure love. Ideas and inspiration rise exuberantly with the steam. I would love to create a Beaker and Bunsen/Mr. Peabody machine to pipette all of it into a bottle for safekeeping. I could line the bottles up in the bookcase in my studio, ready to be decanted whenever I feel confused, discouraged or in need of direction.

> unexplainable
> whim-trusting
> eccentric bursts
> sudden ideas and turns of the mind
> unreasonable

Life can feel small and inconsequential day-to-day, but the overall story can be glorious. Which is more important? Daydreaming about that novella-in-flash festival in Bath or stopping on the sidewalk to hear the old man's story? My shower-self knows the answer. Everything is sacred, from the passion to create, to the old man on the sidewalk, to sitting quietly to stare out to the sea.

lost at cousin jackie's

THE SKY IS THICK WITH STARS. I can hear the cows' hooves
shuffling in the grass and their breath snorting in the soft
night air. I am lost, happy for the barbed wire fence and the
six-foot grass berms that line the narrow road.

My father's cousin, my first cousin once removed, at least
I think that's what they said. We went over all when I met
him for the first time last week, traveling around the Ring
of Kerry with my mother and my aunt. We visited them all,
the Tarrants in Limerick, the Deneheys in Waterville, finally
finding Jackie in the modern ranch house he'd just built to
replace the old family stucco farmhouse next door, a picture
postcard of old Ireland.

Jackie is middle-aged and single. He has the big head and kind, drooping eyes of my father. A pleasant man, a deliverer of fish.

We all stand in the kitchen. Jackie is genial, with lots of *Ochs* and *Ahhs*, but his laugh freezes on his face when I joke about coming back to marry him, that I'd love to fix up the old, abandoned house. But what would I do with the children, I think quietly to myself. Have I completely lost my mind? Would they live with their father and come to visit me every once in a while? Why am I trying on these ridiculous scenarios?

After I see my mother and aunt off at Shannon Airport, I head back to Cahersiveen on the bus. I have no idea why. I listen to some music in a pub, the long Irish evening daylight stretching eerily towards midnight.

I thumb, mother of God, at my age. Whoever it was drops me off at the foot of what I think is Jackie's road. And now, I am walking up the hill towards Jackie's place, hearing the breath of the cows, everything smelling like loneliness, when the headlights of a car come bouncing up the road behind me.

"Can we help you then?" asks the young man, leaning forward, towards the driver's side window, over the woman at the wheel. "Are ya lost? Where ya headed? Och, well now, Jackie's off on his route. You can stay the night with us if you like."

I climb in the back seat. The old car smells of peat and cigarettes. "I'm Jimmy Fitzgerald, but they call me Jimmy Caper because my grandfather came back from a trip to America with the word."

We drive past the old stucco farmhouse, then Jackie's ranch, and head up the next rise to a little house with no lights. I sit in their tiny living room and eat the ham and cookies they put out. We watch a movie with John Wayne and Raquel Welch on a small TV. I sleep in my clothes on a little bed off the kitchen and leave before dawn, wondering if I've lost my mind.

lacrimae rerum

My changes at mid-life were paroxysms —
convulsive, belly-wrenching
gut-run warp spasms
meta-morph, neither man nor beast,
my wing span surprised me
and like any bird trapped inside,
I flapped wildly,
unintentionally damaging my former home
lacrimae rerum
tears shed for future and past lives.
Oh, old friend, we last spoke in your dining room
almost twenty years ago now
when I confided to you that I had kissed a man —
not my husband, but a man,
which was causing my life to unravel.
Before that, we had spent hours and days together,
drinking tea and daydreaming of cottages in France.
But when I told you about kissing the man,
you said all married people are like brothers and sisters
and that all I really wanted was Change.
I winced at the sting and we never spoke again —
you, steady in your kitchen and your sunporch
and me, spinning off into unknown worlds
of pain and exhilaration.

Until now.
Both grandmothers,
we have found each other
on an internet filament
that reaches across geography
and past lives
and our conversation picks up
where it left off
with talk of herb gardens
and bicycling to buy groceries.

on the boardwalk

KATHRYN STRUGGLES to tie her shoe and yet easily twirls
her umbrella like Gene Kelly, crooning all the lyrics to *Singin'
in the Rain*. The grandkids swim in the freezing Atlantic. A
lady passes, then turns and stops to chat. She speaks french
and had a career as a journalist. I think we must have crossed
paths in another life. Her last name was Chabrier, like the
composer, she said. Looked him up when I got home. He
wanted to be a composer, but his family made him study
law. Before he died of syphilis, he wrote very innovative
and original music because he had no training and was not
constrained by all the rules. He influenced Debussy, Ravel,
Satie and all the rest. His best friend was Edouard Manet.
Oh! To have been a mouche on the wall! And let's hear it for
a lack of training! I've been scanning thirty-year-old pictures
of the kids into the computer so I can toss the albums. I won't
be around when everything on the computer will have to
be teleported to a moon of Jupiter. Life is collapsible, like a
toy spyglass. Perhaps I will send away for that certificate to
be a Celtic Priestess so I can perform ancient druidic rites
at weddings. The piano keys tilt like Soutine's buildings in
Céret. I haven't made a pineapple upside down cake in years.
Maybe tomorrow. Later that day, I walk along the boardwalk
- fit bits, clanking halyards, hovering drones, an old man with
elbows bent, pointing skyward as counterweights against
the sinking posture of old age, dogs pulling on leashes, iced
coffees, sugar cones, an oversized brimmed hat strolls east
towards the ocean, flapping in the breeze.

november fields

I HAVE TRAVELED TO THESE NEW YORK HILLS to help my baby survive the birth of her first baby. My own birthing of babies, which seems like ages ago, now feels like yesterday.

I leave her to nurse little Egan, and head up the hill in the late afternoon mist to Aunt Carrie and Uncle Ray's house to dump the compost that has collected in the bucket on the kitchen counter since the baby's arrival on Saturday.

Sloshing up the muddy road, I glance back at the broad, muted fields that sweep down to the Hudson.

I take my sweet time, past the dried fields of corn and meadows of wild growth, drooped and waiting for the first snows.

I empty my bucket into the compost bin — useless bits of rotten vegetables, coffee grounds and eggshells will become next spring's wealth.

Carrie and Ray's garden is an orderly tangram of bolt-fastened raised beds, meticulously cleared and waiting for April's excitement. Theirs is a tidy sort of farming, a far cry from the jumble of wilted tomatoes, cold-hardened peppers and once blissful zinnias that are scattered around our place, frozen in mid-sentence like Pompeian survivors surprised by frost, not falling ash.

I take the long way home, along the mowed path through the fields and thickening dusk. A rabbit darts out onto the grass path. We are equally startled.

Sky color is beginning to blend with earth, making it difficult to see where one begins and the other ends.

I scan the fields for deer, hoping I'll get lucky.

A wren startles me out of my concentration, and I laugh aloud at my jumpiness. I stop to examine a carcass by the side of the path. Intestines and bloated lungs attached to a backbone are all that is left of a surprise encounter.

It has taken me a long life to relish muted colors and low-clouded skies. Back then, I only wanted sun. I had no appreciation for the fading or the lame.

I wonder if my Cecily will be lonely out here with her new baby and her long days, but I realize it is my own loneliness that scares me.

I am supposed to be coming up with my name as a grandmother. The choice, which seems so important at times, doesn't worry me now as I walk along these ancient hills that have cradled so many babies and so many grandmothers; each generation thinking they are the first to plant.

We all press ahead with new boundaries and brave plans, never imagining it will all be plowed under by our children and grandchildren.

i'll fly away

So, YOU MIGHT REMEMBER how I was telling you about my sister's funeral, which happened during all the Covid madness and even though she didn't die of the virus (at least that's what the assisted living place told us), we had to abide by all the restrictions, you know, no church service, no wake to speak of, just a smattering of family standing awkwardly around the open casket of my older sister, the third of four sisters who are all pretty good-looking, but she was the prettiest — always dressed to the nines, everything just right, with the special silver necklace and the matching scarves and tasteful silk blouses. She certainly knew how to present a polished and professional look — more than any of the rest of us! So you can imagine that everyone agreed how wonderful it was that she could be made so pretty again, lying in her white satin bed, wearing all her favorite jewelry and her hair just right, dressed in red, her favorite color and looking so peaceful. But funny, I can't remember now if she was holding rosary beads, which is the custom, but she probably was, because she adored tradition and custom and decorum and of course her husband, who perhaps leans a bit heavy in general on how things look, had arranged that every detail be picture-perfect and had the clout or the pull or whatever, to first of all, arrange a very nice funeral so quickly, but also to arrange an open casket on the first day, with ashes (I've read there is a huge back up on

cremations!) in a lovely Chinese vase on the next. He made
sure that everything was smooth and seamless — so much so
that I felt we were part of a Fellini film when we all drove in
a parade of separate cars to St. Mary's cemetery to gather at
the gravesite of my father and mother and younger brother,
who died of epilepsy when he was only only twenty five — so
young, but he had had a tough go of it, ending up in a room in
a lonely boarding house, a fact that broke my mother's heart
and of course we all wonder if that grief is really what killed
my father less than a year later, but you know, to tell you

the truth, nobody really knows about these things and God knows, every family has their dramas and their sagas, their triumphs and their failures, but back to Fellini, when we all pulled up in our caravan of cars to that beautiful cemetery, we were greeted by friends standing like Greek statues in small clusters. I couldn't help but think of the Caryatids that my sister loved so much, being a student and then a teacher of Latin and Greek, and as I was saying, standing like Greek statues in front of that spectacular house-sized outcropping of granite which graces that section of the cemetery. A white marble statue of the Pietà sat atop the rock, glowing in the late May sun, surrounded by faithful friends, scattered about, buffeted by occasional outbursts of wind, in silent witness to a death — a frozen gathering of Caryatids.

The priest did not come, for fear of Covid, but a very nice gentleman, whom we had never met, gave a very beautiful personal tribute to my sister, which was pretty amazing, seeing as he had never met her (such a great gift, don't you think?) and then we all sang *I'll Fly Away*, that beautiful old gospel hymn that says 'When I die, Hallelujah, by and by, I'll fly away', such a marvelous message for my sister who had the good fortune to slip away in her sleep (a gift from the angels, they say) before her dementia totally destroyed her and all of us, and so it ended up being a joyous celebration of death and flying and I have to say, I was so distracted by the Caryatids, the Pietà, the wind, the Chinese vase, the eulogy, the singing, and well, the beauty of the whole thing that it was all I could think about, and I wanted desperately to capture the scene with my iPhone, but thankfully was aware enough to feel in my still-living bones how inappropriate it would be to take a picture of such fine friends come to mourn with us, but I have to say, because I was not able to take that photograph, I will never be done with trying to describe the scene.

funeral arrangements

Women know how to put on a funeral, don't they?
They kill the fatted calf,
cut the canapés,
brew the coffee and write the glowing articles for
the ones who died first,
who benefitted from a well-planned service,
with readings, speakers, songs and accolades;
a day filled
with fond memories and tearful goodbyes.
But what of the old women?
There will be no one left to tell the world
how well they said goodbye
to all their friends and lovers.
They will go quietly
amidst the rush of younger lives.

at the kitchen sink

Over the years, she had become lost
amongst the silverware and the glasses.
She was now a stranger to herself.

last call

CAFÉ BEAUJOLAIS, the lights are dim, but she doesn't need 'em anyway, just closes her eyes and plays. The crowd at the bar isn't listening but she's used to that. Her cigarette burns low in the ashtray. She thinks about how she got here.

"Learn this, you know, man, like over a two-five-one, up chromatically and then you could do just the left-hand voicings, or the left hand could play the bass line inversions — so then you could take it, you know, approach the C startin' off. You could do little arpeggios or pentatonics, like a B flat pentatonic over a C minor, that's gonna sound slightly out - kind of a tritone substitution sharp eleven — a Lydian sound, y'know?"

Lydian, Dorian, Phrygian…I wonder if they played jazz in the Middle Ages.

"Right hand voicings — that makes it kind of interesting!"

My eyes wander to the smear of a freshly killed mosquito on the wall above the piano.

"So, the first one you should do is those mixed voicings, you know, the shells on the left. Or just practice the blues in every key. But the thing is, you don't wanna just do that, you wanna spread 'em out, see? That's just usin' those same notes, but it sounds better. Do you mind me thinkin' in G Major? Skip every other note, they sound better opened up. Did we do *Green Dolphin Street*? C major seven, up chromatically, two altered pentatonic scales…"

It seems like a dream, yet I know it happened.

"Flat six, the shape of the solo is very angular, scales and targets, scales and triplets."

Fish have scales, like a suit of armor, less drag in the water. Dolphins are mammals though.

"Try this. Comp on *Bluesette*, Bb major."

Poor little, sad little blue Bluesette, don't you cry, don't you fret, you can bet one lucky day you'll waken and your blues will be forsaken.

"Nice progression to learn over a two-five-one. That's so out, man!"

Toots Thielemans played harmonica. Maybe I should try that. Why not?

"Oh yeah, that was obviously E flat — a half step below and a scale step above. Major pentatonic works really well here."

I never think of this without a sigh, y'know what I mean?

"I'm approaching the third, the nine instead of the one, see? Whole step, half step, you know, diminished, you can get shapes out of that. There's only three of 'em too! Like, that would be like, what am I doin'? There's this one, this one, this one. Now if you move any of these, it's the same chord and you could do those for quick fills. God, what would you use over A minor 7 flat five? I love the form of this thing, by the way."

Years later, the melting ice has thinned down her scotch. Hah! chuckling to herself and twisting her face…that's pretty out! Table five requests *All of Me* again. It's late, she thinks, downing her watered-down scotch. Time to head home.

chewing gum man

Remember I was telling you about the man on London's
Millenium Bridge, lying on his side, painting teeny scenes on
dried-up pieces of chewing gum stuck in the cracks? He gave
me his card. *The Chewing Gum Man*. Tourists paid no atten-
tion. Is he at peace? Does he ever wonder if he's taken a wrong
path? And what makes any of us do what we do anyway? I
squirrel away at my computer with writing projects, wonder-
ing if I should get back to the guitar, or that my painting ca-
reer is dead in the water, the days slipping by while my knees
become more and more arthritic and threads of memory fray.
Terrifying, when I think of my mother languishing away for
10 years, her mind gone. What's the point? Maybe I'll head
up to Vermont for a dose of assisted suicide when the time
comes. But I won't know when the time comes.

the unbroken cup

Aunt Joan called this morning, upset, couldn't find the words to say she had broken a cup, needed help sweeping it up. When I got there, she was sitting in her chair, still as a rock, with none of her usual cheeriness. She watched, silent, as I swept up the few pieces she had missed. I sat down, very close to her and asked if she was doing OK. I'm just hungry, she answered. She had been afraid to go into the kitchen area. I told her to sit, that I would wait on her — not her favorite. Bananas, cereal, grapes, nuts, a bit of yogurt, milk, hot water in the unbroken cup. As we spoke of yesterday's lunch at church and the birds outside her window, her lost-ness and stillness started to dissipate. But she was sad. She sat in her kitchen chair. I stood behind her hugged her from above. Something about the angle of the embrace broke my heart — me standing above her, holding her in my arms, like the Pietà. We both cried, for different reasons I suppose; Joan, because old age was gaining on her; I, because I knew that for whatever reason, I had never experienced this with my mother. My mother's kid sister was teaching me about love.

dream cathedral

HALFWAY THROUGH one of my in-town walks, I stop at a favorite spot along the river. I sit in one of the cheap plastic Adirondack chairs left behind by some fellow pilgrim. I sit in silence to stare out over the water.

At low tide the marsh grass defines inviting pathways for muddy treks to distant mudflats. In winter, higher king tides rush past the turbulent cut between two jetties. The deep channel in the middle of the river stealthily drives tons of water back upstream, the tide seeping higher and higher, until it edges silently to the foot of my holy wall.

This is not a place of turbulence. The slow steady rise of the water swallows the long upright blades of grass,
   slowly submerging them all. Spikes adapt and turn supple in graceful and humble response. Like a full head of long hair lingering in a hot bath, the grass waves this way and that, gently pushed by invisible moon-driven bulges of water.

This is not the boardwalk where tourists and townspeople stroll. Nor is it the beach, where we swim or read a book. This place is a secret, unnoticed weed-strewn spot, a gravel patch, held safe from the tides by a still-sturdy stone wall. The water is calm here, with a view that sweeps out to the jetties and sun-splashed islands on the horizon.

A dream cathedral for all seasons.

non-sense

She had always been able to hear
the smell of burning leaves and taste
the wonder of the moon. Her eyes
could touch the blare of sirens and her hands could feel the
stars. Her inner ear held
the mysteries of odd flavors and she always tried not to smell
or hear the sorrow in the
color red. She couldn't help but taste the
backdrop of phragmites blowing in the
evening wind and her nose sensed colonies of thirsty eyes,
listening, listening for the truth.

walking backwards

SHE WALKED OUT the back door of her perfectly comfortable, but rather depressing memory care unit, looking for home; past the sea where she had scattered her second husband, thinking of his gift for touch; further inland, into a dark forest, where she remembered being lost and then found. She kept walking, towards her first husband and their dear children and grandchildren, now grown, then on to her days of lipstick and fancy dinners, piano lessons and ice skating on the pond in the growing darkness, of bicycles and ice cream cones, until she came to little hat-shaped boats, made from aluminum foil, drifting, drifting down the little stream behind her house.

mudlarking at the beauport

THE HARBOR IS STILL, the air thick with a reluctant fog. A solitary old woman, dressed in a long black coat and a red hat, walks along the low tide line, head lowered, inspecting the narrow beach, bending occasionally to pick up shiny little bits of sea glass. She pecks intently at the ground, inspecting, deciding, pocketing some pieces, throwing others back into the sea. Crows and seagulls drift about, lazily calling to one another, following her closely while keeping watch for any glimmering object or stray clam. The immortal infinity between water and sky makes flight seem possible. A wind comes up, gentle at first, then stronger, sweeping away the reluctant fog. The lady walks along the water's edge, propelled by the billowings of her dark coat. Whenever she stops to look more closely at a glinting something-or-other, the birds, now multiplied, all rush to her, gathering 'round to see what she has discovered. She is lost in a cloud of birds. She seems to be one of them. The birds swirl up in a sudden gust. The lady grabs for her hat too late, the wind spinning it high over the water. She squawks in dismay. A quick-thinking crow swoops, snatches the hat in its beak, circles back and drops it on the beach at the lady's feet. She bends low, places her prize red hat on her head, then arches her back, spreading her arms wide in jubilation. She looks up now at the swarm of shrieking birds, her coat undulating in appreciation. Slowly, slowly she rises with it, up, up into the crow-filled sky and flies off to sea, leaving her red hat on the beach.

nine lives

Just like a cat, I want nine lives
I wanna let new journies materialize
Slinkin' around wherever I can
from a hot tin roof to a fryin' pan

Just like a fish in the deep blue sea
I wanna let the water wash over me
Swim around where it's dark and cool
in that big black ocean swimming pool

Just like a snake, I'm gonna shed some skin
Gonna think things over, Rebegin.
Slide on out of the Promised Land
Ooze on over to the Devil's Hand

Just like a bird, I'm gonna fly free
Float through the clouds naturally
Swoop down low and buzz my friends
The aviary happiness never ends.

Why don't you just face it
Whatever you do.
This life's a wild place
This life's a zoo

lyrics from Nine Lives, the title track
from a collection of original songs

smoke and mirrors

Watercolor is slippery
unruly, seeping, uncontrollable,
pigment blooming
in unwanted directions,
weeping into unexpected crevices.
Sometimes, she looks deeper
into the mirror
searching for her true self,
but sees only a stranger.

she paints lips, nostrils
then eyes,
outward looking
wondering what they look like to the
world

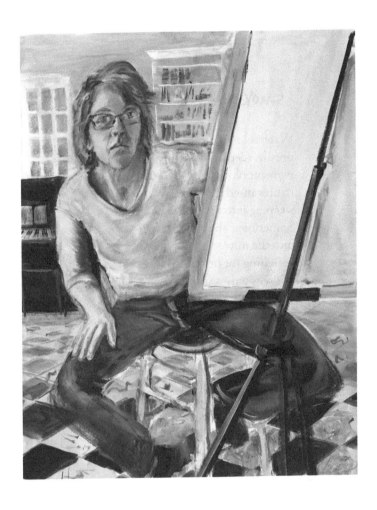

Kate Sullivan likes to play around with words, music and pictures. She has written and illustrated the children's books *On Linden Square* (Sleeping Bear Press) and *What Do You Hear?* (Schiffer Books).

She has sung chansons at **NYC Mme Tussaud's Wax Museum** and her fugue-ish *Fugitum est* was performed at **Carnegie Hall** by **The Kremlin Chamber Orchestra** as part of their tribute to Mozart. She also likes to paint ostriches and play the musical saw to impress people.

Her poems and paintings have appeared in *Flash Frog, Loud Coffee Press, Sleet Magazine, Rush Literary Magazine, Dillydoun Review* and *Writers.com*, among others.

She can be reached through **sullyarts.com**.

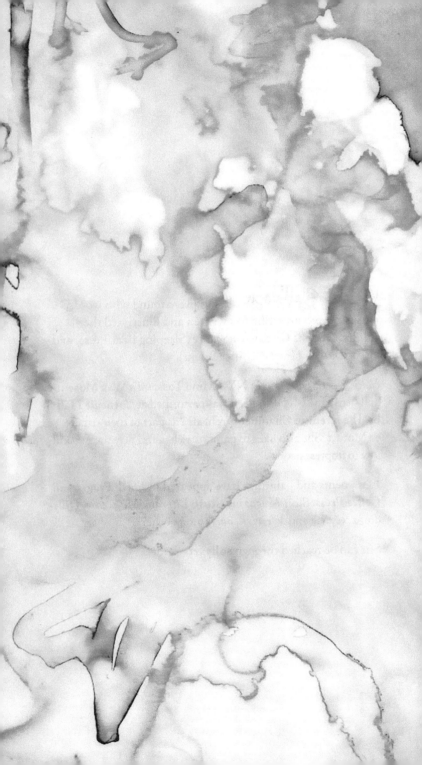